ANGEL MAGIC

DEDICATION

This book is dedicated to Madeleine Montalban from
whom I first received these teachings and Ilse Ferguson
who effected the introduction, and to my lovely
daughter who has always been my inspiration.

Special thanks to my dear friend David Workman,
without whose help this would never have happened,
and also to Don my partner for his help.

ANGEL MAGIC

THE PAULINE ART OF RITUAL AND MAGIC

Betty St Pourçain

Published by SILVERDALE BOOKS
An imprint of Bookmart Ltd
Registered number 2372865
Trading as Bookmart Ltd
Blaby Road
Wigston
Leicester LE18 4SE

© 2005 D&S Books Ltd

D&S Books Ltd
Kerswell,
Parkham Ash, Bideford
Devon, England
EX39 5PR

e-mail us at:-
enquiries@d-sbooks.co.uk

This edition printed 2005

ISBN 1-84509-061-6

DS0136. Angel Magic

Creative Director: Sarah King
Editor: Anna Southgate
Project editor: Judith Millidge
Designer: 2H Design

Set in Bembo and Serlio

Printed in China

1 3 5 7 9 10 8 6 4 2

CONTENTS

FOREWORD

These teachings were first given to me in the early 1980s and have been built upon since that time, although I did not feel ready to teach them universally until now. We are all under the influence of the 'seventh ray', the 'ceremonial order of magic' and we have access to many Divine tools to help us on our spiritual journey. It is time to flow with energy and for us all to become 'Shamans' – technicians of the sacred. To this end, I have decided to write this book with the help of my friend, David Workman, and I trust many people will feel the benefit of allowing the Angel Light to flood into their lives. It is all a simple matter of self-identification.

Approximately every 2,000 years, as a result of the great cycle of the Zodiac, the energy of the ray which influences the planet changes. There are in total seven great rays of energy. The last one in the Piscean Age was 'devotion and idealism' – Christianity was born under this ray and spread to 37% of the world's population. These are rays which guide Man's evolution. At present humankind needs to expand its

mind to recognise the order and magic all around us, the ceremony in nature and the Divine tools with which we are being presented. The Angels work with the rays, and the energy in the great ray assists especially with Angel Magic.

Are you a spiritual being having a human experience? Or do you see yourself as a human being having the odd spiritual experience? The former is the reality and we need to make this connection and identify with our spiritual natures. Using Angel Light is just one of many ways of realising our potential and allowing divine energy to flow into our lives. Using divine power makes life much easier: it is a support system that will never let you down. Our lives are restrained by the limitations we impose on ourselves – now is the time for freedom. Free yourself of negative thought and walk freely into the Light. I invite the readers of this book to accept this challenge: Change your life for the better.

Betty St Pourçain – July 2004

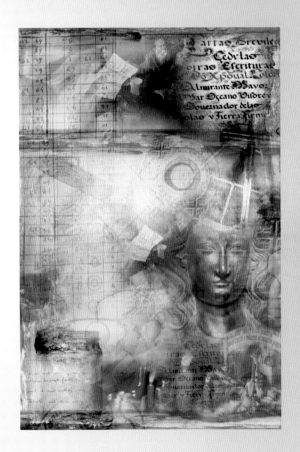

An Introduction to Angel Magic

Magic is the ability to use the natural law of the universe in order to bring about change in your life and in the lives of others. We all have this ability, it is just a question of knowing how to use it. Firstly, we need to understand that all is energy – everything in the manifested universe is energy vibrating at different speeds, different frequencies. Even the solid, dense forms we perceive are an illusion; it is just that the vibration is so slow, it gives the impression of being solid. Everything comes from the mind of God or the 'creative source' so real creation takes place in the higher realms, in the dimensions of a more subtle energy. All of us have a spark of the Divine within us, we are, at our best, co-creators with the Divine. We are able to create our own reality. Angel Magic gives us the chance to use this natural ability. It is the use of the natural law with the addition of the power and love of the angelic realms, the great archangels and the whole of the 'angelic and elemental kingdom'. With Angel Magic we also use the sacred shapes, sounds, colours, crystals and languages (scripts): the communication

system of the 'spiritual hierarchy of the planet'. It has been said that 'the end of all true philosophy and magic is to arrive at a knowledge of the Creator through knowledge of the Created World'.

The first thing we need to do is to become aware of the magical universe in which we live, and of our own part within it. We need to appreciate that everything in the cosmos comes from the one creative source. This source is responsible for all the diversity of creation. We need to know and recognise that every life form has a built-in need for survival. Pure magic has a respect for all life and knows each life form has its own part to play in the cosmic drama and must not be harmed. All this life is held together by a universal mind. In magic we learn to tap into this universal mind. The world is full of elemental energy – the elementals work as builders of form – and in some cases we can use this elemental energy to build what we want.

We can create for ourselves as long as we do not deprive or interfere with the needs of others. As a user of Angel Magic your responsibility is great; if you misuse this power, the Law of Karma or cause and effect comes into action. Energy itself is neither good nor evil: it is in the mind and intention of the aspiring magician that this natural power can be turned into a source for good or evil.

Magic in its highest form is invoking the power of the Creator and bringing it down into manifested life. Use your magic creatively with love and good intention and the angels will be happy and eager to work with you, to help yourself and others.

Ceremonial Order and Magic

At this present stage the planet basks in the energy of the seventh ray, Ceremonial Order and Magic. This ray is ruled by the ascended master St. Germain and the Angel of Spiritual Magic, Gabriel. These two, working together, seek to bring about the greatest alchemy of all, changing man from a material to a spiritual being. We are all beings of energy, vibrating at different rates or different frequencies; as the energy of the ray pours down, it has a great influence on our growth. Many ancient belief systems refer to this universal energy in different terms — as 'Chi' by the Chinese, or 'Prana' by Hindus. Each great stream of energy which stimulates the evolution of man is presided over by an angelic presence who constantly works and directs for the good of humanity. The seventh ray stimulates the magical aspect of our creation, and using rite and ceremony, we are able to tap into a reservoir of spiritual, angelic energy to help us achieve our goals. Each ray has its own colour: for this one the colour is violet and the use of this colour has the effect of dispelling negative situations and negativity. There are angels of each ray and the angels working with the seventh ray are known as the 'violet angels of transmutation'. This period of time in the history of our planetary evolution is one of great potential for magic. We are able to connect with this magical spiritual energy and use it to re-invent ourselves and to gain all the material, emotional, mental and spiritual gifts we crave for. We need to use this magical energy with reverence and respect and not exclusively for ourselves.

THE PAULINE ART

The Pauline Art is an ancient system of practical ritual magic based on the age-old Kabbala. This system held that one God, the Universal Creator, had subdivided His powers into a hierarchy of 'spiritual beings of light', 'archangels' and 'angels'. As far as our universe is concerned, He appointed a ruling angel to each planet, with other angels for the two zodiacal divisions of each sign.

MAN'S EVOLUTION

Since time began, these angels were appointed to teach evolving Man the holy law, which meant not just the Ten Commandments, but the whole theory of how the universe was linked together from the highest (the Creator) to the lowest (the first protoplasm of primeval ponds) in one interwoven mesh. The idea was that Man evolved from this protoplasm through re-incarnation and would, in time, become a fully physically evolved human. His rudimentary brain needed tuition in order to fulfil the plan, however, along the lines that 'Man should develop into an intelligent, instructed human with a soul, and from then on, through countless incarnations, learn all that God knew'. As he evolved, Man was to be instructed by the

planetary angels, and would come under the dominion of
each one. It was to this end that the Creator 'set the stars
in the heavens and gave them the word of command over
Man'. (Madeline Montalban.)

Man would be kept under the guidance of the planets
until he was sufficiently evolved to exercise his own free
will. On reaching such a level, the teaching angels would
then divulge their own secrets, thereby making Man equal
in knowledge to themselves. Eventually Man would reach
the status of angelhood himself, at which point he would
be absorbed into the body of God and reborn again, this
time as an angel and given dominion over some new
planet in some new universe, to teach in turn, the beings
that were evolving from protoplasmic matter as Man
himself had done. In its purest form, this is the art of
astrology, and is the very basis of the Pauline Art. For in
astrology we learn how the planets influence the lives and
destinies of Man, in order that each human may know and
use the wisdom taught by the angels of each planet.

The Pauline Art of Ritual and Magic is not a 'black art'. It
enables you to make the best of yourself and your talents.
It gives rewards for efforts made. No magic spell can bring
you anything you have not earned, either in this or a

previous life, but it will enable you to make the very utmost of God and to expand your life. When you need a miracle, it will be there, for the angels never fail those who are earnestly trying. Many of us have good deeds 'in the bank', from previous lives and have earned more than we know, and these credits in the astral bank can be drawn upon when we really need help. They are all on record. But to prove big truths, we must first prove small ones and that is the intention of this book.

At times all of us have to undergo difficult periods in our lives. If we did not have difficulties, troubles and sorrows, if we were not provided with something to overcome and *to learn from*, we would make no progress at all. We would be undeveloped human beings.

Humanity must learn and strive upwards to win the soul and then to proceed, by degrees, to mastership of the planetary effects and eventually to angelhood, after which, re-incarnation in the human form would cease. Then each of us would be re-absorbed into the Supreme Creator from thence to be re-born as Angels to teach inhabitants of new universes, which are always being created. Ours is but one of many worlds, our universe but one of a myriad others. Such according to the Pauline Art, was the master plan of the Creator. The more we learn, the more the

Angels help us upwards and the less effect the planets have to afflict us. We become the masters of fate and no longer the victims of it.

If one traces the birth of the Manifested Universe from the Sea of Potential to the Creative Mind

> **THOUGHT ➡ LIGHT ➡ RESONANCE ➡ VIBRATION ➡ SOUND ➡ COLOUR ➡ FORM.**

This is the Creative Matrix in the Higher Levels forming archetypes which ultimately lead to all aspects of Manifested Creation. We can tap into this creative stream at a higher level and through this bring about changes in manifestation here. If one traces the chain of communication again it emerges from the Great Mind in the form of electrical impulses, tele-thought, then the language of pictographs, which developed into the Celestial Scripts, Sacred Languages, Hieroglyphs and finally our own common form of language. This is why visualisation is useful and important in magical work because it links with a pictorial rather than verbal way of thinking, so providing access to a higher realm. If you create something in your mind in the same way as an artist would create a picture, taking time and trouble and effort till it was perfect, your chance of bringing that 'picture' into manifestation is very high. The use of sacred language in magical ritual is very effective (see page 46).

All shapes and numbers are potent tools, as shapes carry a specific energy and the numbers 7, 9, 10 and 12 are particularly significant for us (see page 56).

There are also correspondences and relationships between planets – use their power and energy with your intentions (see page 39).

THE ANGELIC
KINGDOMS

Angels are messengers of God ('angelos' is Greek for messenger) and they were intended to teach God's Law to evolving Man, as well as the whole theory of how the Universe was linked together from the highest to the lowest in one interwoven mesh.

FIRST HIERARCHY
THE ASPECTS OF GOD

The Seraphims surround the throne of God and are regulators of the movement of the heavens. They have purifying and enlightening powers and inhabit the first cause, the initial and pure intention of the one God who seeks to know Himself through the outing of all existence. Seen as holy spirits with six wings, they are constantly singing God's praises. Depictions of the flames of devoted love, they are the Hierarchy who best depict the devoted love of the Creator or the Creative Source.

The Cherubims are heavenly counsellors and guardians of the Light. They have the power of knowing. They inhabit the sphere of the fixed stars – the wisdom of God found by seekers of eternal truth. Pictured with four faces and four wings, they are usually golden yellow or blue, and hold an open book or scroll.

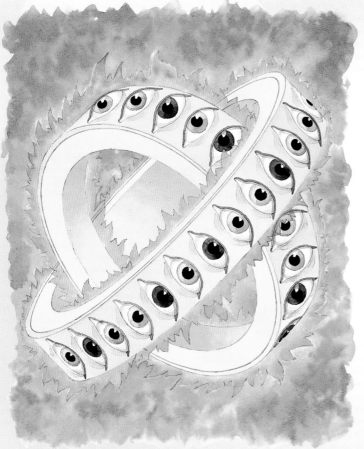

The Thrones are companion angels of all the planets. They represent divine majesty, divine priests and princes of the courts of heaven. They inhabit the fiery wheels of the throne of God. They are pictured as wheels with the many eyes of all-seeing wisdom, or perhaps as figures holding flowers or the scales of justice. They symbolise true majesty, and the strong and mighty will that supports Divinity.

SECOND HIERARCHY
THE ADMINISTRATORS OF
GOD'S CREATION

The Dominions assist in the integration of the material and spiritual worlds. They may be crowned and hold an orb and sceptre, or cross or sword to symbolise the balanced force behind creation. They represent the superiority of wisdom over intellect and govern the natural world and the elements.

The Virtues assimilate the will of God and enfold Mother Earth in divine energies. They are associated with heroic deeds and miracles performed on Earth. They may carry a sword or sceptre and shield to symbolise courage. They are shining and brilliant.

The Powers carry flaming swords to protect humanity, and help anchor God's divine plan for our planet and bring humanity a vision of unity with all Creation. They are associated with the imposition of the will of God and prevent the forces of darkness from dominating in the world, so protecting and guiding lost souls.

THIRD HIERARCHY
THE MINISTERING ANGELS IN HUMAN AFFAIRS

The Principalities are the guardians of large groups such as cities and nations, or leaders in military, religious and political spheres. They monitor the destiny and Karma of nations. They also watch over the leaders of the angelic hosts.

The Archangels are great beings of light and love and the leaders of the angelic hosts. Despite their position in the hierarchy, archangels are chief angels who attend the throne of God and reveal God's presence to human beings.

THE BEST-KNOWN ARCHANGELS

GABRIEL, whose name means 'God is my strength', rules the spirits of men. Divine alchemist and angel of magic, he commands spiritual vision. He is angel of the astral and heavenly worlds. He is associated with the Moon, water, emotions and the feminine side of Nature.

MICHAEL THE MERCIFUL, whose name means 'who is of God' or 'perfect of God'. He is the angel of repentance, righteousness, forgiveness and the mysteries of the Light. The protector and transmuter of the negative, he is patron of Israel, head of the heavenly host and close to both God and humanity. Michael is a truly royal angel. He works with Metatron and radiant Light represented by the Sun (the Solar Logos), as well as with the law of magnetism. Michael is our protector too, as long as we seek to live within God's law.

RAPHAEL THE DIVINE PHYSICIAN, whose name means 'God has healed', triumphs over despair, disease and wounds. Angel of healing and patron of travellers, he is Chief Divine Messenger and an angel of great ingenuity. Raphael takes requests to the appropriate source. If you are unsure which Angel to call upon for specific help, call upon Raphael to re-direct your call to the appropriate angel. He is an Angel of great tenderness and also helps with the animals.

URIEL, whose name means 'fire of God', denotes wisdom, tolerance, development and sustenance. He is guardian of the new spiritual age and keeper of the gates of Zion. He teaches us truth and helps us to step out of individuality and into wholeness and unity.

THE BEST-KNOWN ANGELS.

The angels are beings of light who assist the archangels in helping all areas of Creation. They heal, illuminate, purify and transform. They work with all of Creation as builders of form under the guidance of the archangels. They are always happy to be of service if you invoke their help.

ANAEL is the angel of higher joy, beauty and peace. He brings joy and happiness into your life. You can also call on him for justice, when you feel you are not being treated fairly or when you need help in a matter connected with civil justice or your dealings with others. His power works well with crystal energy (see page 59).

CASSIEL, the angel connected to the law of cause and effect, who helps to deal with long-term Karma. He enables you to climb out of whatever situation you find yourself in, with true aspiration and effort.

LUMIEL, the angel for the protection of soul, body, emotions and mind. He protects the soul from separation and disempowerment; the body from ill health; and the mind and emotions from damage and negative vibrations.

METATRON highest of all the angels, he is a prophet, close to God and surrounded by the Seraphim. He is the highest angel in the Kabbalistic 'Tree of Life' and is sometimes known as Phanuel.

SACHIEL, the angel of good fortune who works with Jesus. He is the angel of abundance: call on him when you need material help.

SAMAEL protects in times of danger, such as war or terror. Call on him for power, strength and bravery. He is also good when having to face negative psychic problems.

SANDALPHON, the angel of the Earth, the guardian spirit. The chief and prototype of all guardian angels, he is the tallest angel.

To complete the picture of the hierarchies, we must not forget the other levels of consciousness. These levels are modes or phases of the One Consciousness.

Consciousness is dormant but retentive in the Mineral Kingdom, sleeps in the Plant Kingdom, dreams in the Animal Kingdom and awakens in Humanity. Humanity, although individualised, contains the aggregate of all previous phases of evolution.

The Elemental Kingdoms

THE ELEMENTAL KINGDOM

Angel Magic utilises the power and significance of the Zodiac and the Elementals who work under the guidance of the Angels. Their power and energy help to focus one's attention. Maximum dedication and effort obtains maximum results.

Sylph

Salamander

Undine

Gnome

The Elementals are the builders of form, who assist the angels in their work of constructing, modifying and retaining form. Each group has a king or ruler, and is aligned to particular quarters and elements, as follows:

ELEMENTAL	KING	QUARTER	ELEMENT
Sylphs of the Air	Paralda	East	Air
Salamanders of Fire	Djinn	South	Fire
Undines of Water	Nixsa	West	Water
Gnomes of the Earth	Gnob	North	Earth

There are guiding angels assigned to many things, such as planets, elements, days of the week and zodiacal signs. They also have 'call signs' and 'ray colours' assigned to them. You will need to be aware of this information when you are working your rituals or calling for angelic help.

The following chart should bring them into perspective.

ANGEL	QUARTER	ELEMENT	COLOUR
Michael	South	Fire	Red
Raphael	East	Air	Yellow
Gabriel	West	Water	Blue
Uriel	North	Earth	Green

DAYS OF THE WEEK	
Monday	
Tuesday	
Wednesday	
Thursday	
Friday	
Saturday	Ca
Sunday	

The Role of the Planets

(Neptune is not used here.)

There are correspondences and relationships between the Sun, Moon and planets and you can call upon their power and energy to further your intentions.

Jupiter: for ambition, general success, benevolence, abundance and career success.

Moon: for the astral world, astral travel and knowledge, safe journeys and feminine things.

Venus: for beauty.

Mercury: for business success, communication, building bridges and learning.

Saturn: for esoteric knowledge, study, exams and understanding of Karma.

Jupiter and the Sun: for regained youth, health and harmony, anything connected with the home.

Mars: for military power and discord.

ANGEL	ZODIAC	PLANET
Samael	Aries & Scorpio	Mars
Anael	Taurus & Libra	Venus
Raphael	Gemini & Virgo	Mercury
Gabriel	Cancer	Moon
Michael	Leo	Sun
Sachiel	Sagittarius & Pisces	Jupiter
Cassiel	Capricorn	Saturn
Uriel	Aquarius	Uranus

THE ANGEL MAGIC SYMBOLS AND CALL SIGNS

Michael *Colour: Blue*

DAY	CALL SIGN	PLANET	ZODIAC	ZODIAC 2
Monday				
	Stella/lunar corona	Waxing moon	Sign of Cancer	

Samael *Colour: n/a*

DAY	CALL SIGN	PLANET	ZODIAC	ZODIAC 2
Tuesday				
	Upright sword	Symbol of Mars	Sign of Scorpio	Sign of Aries

Raphael *Colour: Yellow*

DAY	CALL SIGN	PLANET	ZODIAC	ZODIAC 2
Wednesday				
	Bird's head	Symbol of Mercury	Sign of Virgo	Sign of Gemini

Sachiel *Colour: n/a*

DAY	CALL SIGN	PLANET	ZODIAC	ZODIAC 2
Thursday				
	Pact of fortune	Symbol of Jupiter	Sign of Pisces	Sign of Sagittarius

Anael (Haniel) *Colour: n/a*

DAY	CALL SIGN	PLANET	ZODIAC	ZODIAC 2
Friday				
	Chalice cup of happiness	Symbol of Venus	Sign of Libra	Sign of Taurus

Cassiel *Colour: n/a*

DAY	CALL SIGN	PLANET	ZODIAC	ZODIAC 2
Saturday				
	Jacob's ladder	Symbol of Saturn	Sign of Capricorn	

Uriel *Colour: Green*

DAY	CALL SIGN	PLANET	ZODIAC	ZODIAC 2
Saturday				
	Lightning flash	Symbol of Uranus	Sign of Aquarius	

Michael *Colour: Red*

DAY	CALL SIGN	PLANET	ZODIAC	ZODIAC 2
Sunday				
	Golden crown of royalty	Symbol of the Sun	Sign of Leo	

Solar Logos/Sign of Leo

Below are the angel's personal call signs in greater detail:

 Gabriel: the stellar-lunar corona

 Samael: the drawn upright sword

 Raphael: the bird's head

 Sachiel: the pact of fortune

 Anael: the chalice cup of happiness

 Cassiel: the Jacob's ladder

 Uriel: the lightning flash

 Michael: the golden crown of royalty

Using the Angels' Call Signs

The Call Signs are intimately connected with the vibratory energy of the particular angel that the Call Sign relates to. For example, Gabriel is the Angel of Magic and works with the Ascended Master St. Germain who is Lord of the Seventh Ray, Ceremonial Order and Magic. Gabriel's Call Sign can be used for all magical and alchemical processes. If you wish to transform any area of your life magically, this is the Angel to invoke. Using the Angelic Scripts can make the process more effective. The more effort the individual puts in, the more rewarding the results.

For best results, use the special day of the week; sit for a few minutes and mentally call upon the Angel, then light a candle. Draw the Call Sign on a bit of paper and on the reverse write your request using one of the Sacred Scripts. Place under the candle and allow the candle to burn down. Always remember to thank the Angel and finally burn the paper using the flame from the candle just before its goes out, visualising the smoke rising into the angelic dimensions carrying the request straight to the source.

Angels love beauty, so preparation of the space and adding a few flowers or crystals always helps. I knew someone who actually made images or little models of the Angelic Call Signs out of light wood, cardboard, paper and crystals and found this to be a very effective way of calling for angelic help. Use the symbolism of the call signs to their best effect.

GABRIEL The Stellar-Lunar corona. All things magical, for what appears unattainable (reaching for the moon and stars), for feminie things, the Lunar energy.

SAMAEL The drawn upright sword. For going into battle symbolically, for anything where you might have a fight on your hands. For anything on the cutting edge of life, new innovations – high-powered jobs and so on.

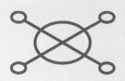

RAPHAEL The bird's head. Information – the bird is seen as the scribe in ancient mythologies, e.g. Thoth as the ibis bird in Egyptian texts. For the written word or knowledge. For flights of fantasy, but also travel that involves flying. For the animal kingdom – for anything connected with helping bird life.

SACHIEL The pact of fortune. For help when pacts and promises have been broken. For all games of chance and luck in general. For universal and planetary changes.

ANAEL The Chalice Cup of Happiness. For spiritual help (the chalice is symbolically perceived as the Holy Grail) and for everything associated with personal or collective happiness.

CASSIEL Jacob's ladder. For effort and achievement in all areas of life (climbing the ladder steadily). For acceptance into particular social groups or circles, for the successful completion of building work on the physical level and for the building of abstract things, like dreams and the fulfilment of hopes and ideas.

URIEL The Lightning Flash. For the unexpected, and sudden, overwhelming enlightenment. For everything connected with electricity and so with power, including power struggles.

MICHAEL The Golden Crown of Royalty. For all things of statuesque proportions; for dealing with the establishment. For the acquisition of gold (in all its meanings), from spiritual transformation to purchasing an item of gold jewellery.

COMMUNICATION
AIDS

Angels respond to beauty. It is therefore beneficial to use colours and crystals in the rituals. Symbols and scripts carry an ancient energy which is invoked and can be very powerful. In a way, it is going back in time to when creation was formed out of the matrix of energies. We tap into the source of this creative energy which enhances the efficacy of the ritual.

The Sacred Languages

Angels respond to Sacred Sounds, hence the use of the Sacred Languages.

The use of sacred language in magical ritual is very effective. There are five sacred languages: Hebrew, Sanskrit, Tibetan, Chinese and Egyptian. The power and magic these languages hold is due to the acoustic vibrations that occur when they are spoken aloud. For Angel Magic I would recommend the use of Hebrew.

For example, 'L, Malkuth, Ve Geburah, Ve Gedulah, Le Ouam,' meaning 'Thou art the Kingdom, the Power and the Glory, Amen'. This invocation or salutation fills your body with astral light and connects you to the higher kingdoms. Use the sacred names of God – there are many – Adonai, Abba, YHWH, El Elohim and many others. You may have a favourite; use it. In the Bible when God spoke to Moses from the Burning Bush, He identified Himself with the words 'Eyeh, Asher, Eyeh', meaning 'I Am That I Am'.

The Sacred Scripts

Sacred scripts are often used in Angel Magic. The Theban and River Scripts given here date back to a time before hieroglyphics and the pictogram scripts used by ancient civilisations. These scripts were used by angels or messengers of God who walked with men. When you use these scripts you link to that energy and open up channels of communication that lie dormant in our bodies for most of the time. These are used to write to the Angels and especially to write the name of the person for whom the ritual is being performed.

Use the Theban and River Scripts to write on the reverse of life protection charts (see page 81) or when making healing squares and talismans (see page 76). Everything responds to the effort you put in. Use these scripts to write to the Angels to invoke for yourself and for others. You will be surprised at the results.

Remember, these scripts are purely based on sound, so unlike our alphabet, where you would use many letters of the alphabet to spell a name, here you may need fewer, as it is the combination of the sounds that is important.

For example, in the river script the name Peter would look like this:

The same example in the Theban Script would look like this:

A further example of how energies work with the sacred scripts is the Mantra of Compassion, written in the ancient language of Sanskrit. When chanted with pure heart, the mantra invokes the Bodhisattva of Compassion – Quan Yin. It is pronounced '*Om mani padme hum.*' Using mantras, music and visualising light and colour always brings Angelic help closer. Angels are Beings of Light and respond to our use of the divine tools. The mantra of compassion can be used to invoke the help of Kuan Yin, the Bodhisattva of Compassion, who is an embodiment of God's Love and Compassion and is also assisted by the myriad of Angels. I would use this mantra in cases of great need, in cases of serious illness and when whole areas of the planet need help, because of natural disasters or war.

The Kodoish, Kodoish Adonai T'sebayoth is a Hebrew mantra which calls together all the People of God, the Spiritual Hierarchy and the Angelic Realms. It gives protection and help.

Quan Yin, literally 'the enlightened one', or Bodhisattva, vowed to remain in the earthly realms and not enter the heavenly worlds until all other living things have completed their own enlightenment and thus become liberated from the pain-filled cycle of birth, death, and rebirth.

THE RIVER SCRIPT

A – broad sounding as in Ay.

B – Be or Bee

D – De of Dee

E – as in where, E or Er

G – hard as in Get

H – hard as in His

I - all I's and e's – sound of ee

J – all J's and Y's
– soft sound as in Ye

K – hard sound as in Cat

L – El

M – Em

N – En

O – as in Cold – O and Oh

P – Pe or Pea

Q – Ku or Queue

R – Ar or R

S – as in Stay

T – Te of Tea

Sh – as in Show

V – use two v's for W
– also U and OO sound

Th – as in There

Z – Zee

THE THEBAN SCRIPT

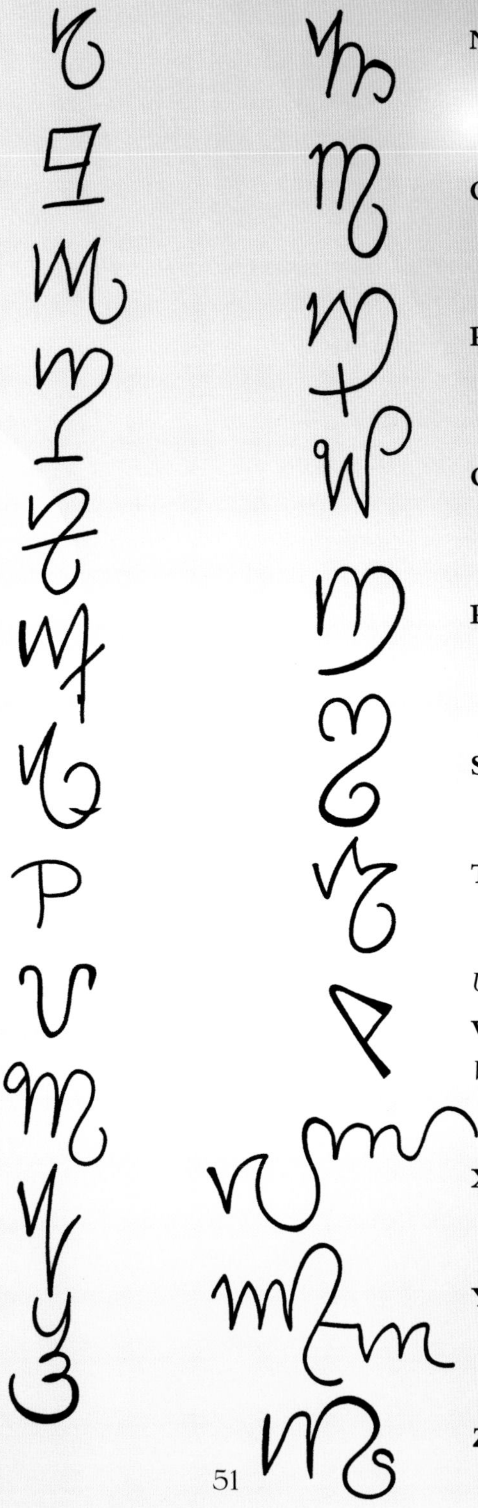

A

B

C

D

E

F

G

H

I

J not used, use I

K

L

M

N

O

P

Q

R

S

T

U not used, use V

V

W not used, use V twice

X

Y

Z

51

INVOKING THE ANGELS:
BOBBY'S STORY

Bobby needed his car to go and do a favour for a friend. The previous day he had also wanted to use the car but the battery was dead and he ended up using a taxi in order to finish his project on time. Giving up was not on the menu for today, however, so he walked to where the car was parked. There was hardly enough power to use the central locking to open the doors, but he was determined to get the engine to fire up. Sitting in the driving seat, he explained to the Universe why he needed the car and invoked the 'Kodoish' mantra. After waiting for a few seconds, he turned the key and the engine sprang into life — so, after thanking the angels for their help, he drove off to help his friend.

This was not the first time that angelic forces had helped him when he had a problem with a car. On a very wet night, he was driving home when a roundabout loomed out of the murk. Braking seemed to have no effect, the car just carried on at the same speed. Taking his hands from the wheel and his foot off the brake pedal, he called to Archangel Michael to help him. The car slowed and moved to the correct lane for his exit onto the roundabout and stopped, ready to set off again when he had recovered his composure. Bobby has always invoked the help of Archangel Michael before travelling at any time.

USEFUL INVOCATIONS USING SACRED SCRIPTS.

Example: 'I invoke the blessings and help of Lord Michael'.

River Script   **Theban Script**

For Lord Uriel   For Lord Uriel

For Lord Raphael.   For Lord Raphael.

For Lord Gabriel.   For Lord Gabriel

Use the Sacred Scripts to write to the Angels. There is a connection of Light between the Scripts and the Angelic Energy which materialises thought.

I know of two friends who write to each other using the Scripts. They say that their friendship has deepened, problems are solved very quickly and even their relationships with their family members have improved considerably.

The use of the Scripts seems to attract an energy of Goodness, Light and Power which permeates through the life of the user. We are reaching a crucial time in the evolution of our planet. I believe we are collectively standing at the threshold of a new dimension of awareness into which we will all move in time. We are being helped by the Spiritual Hierarchies and are being given back many divine tools to help our progression into this higher state of enlightenment. The Angels are very close to us and each Order is carrying out its specific function to help Humanity and all life to reach that perfect stage of unity.

SYMBOLS

The prime sacred shapes are the circle, the triangle, the square, the Star of David and the five-pointed star. Each of these shapes carries with it an acoustic vibration, which can be used by the magician with great success.

The circle represents the total power of God.

The square is for Angel Magic. Use this for all angel work.

The upper triangle (point upwards) is for all spiritual energy work.

The lower triangle (point down) pertains to the physical.

The Star of David represents the physical and spiritual attributes of Man in harmony.

The five-pointed star focuses magical energy and may also be used in healing as the symbol of the human form.

Magic develops your mind and your ingenuity. 'Necessity is the mother of invention', so remember that any symbol you invent to help yourself has true power, and the angels will understand it. In the words of Raphael, 'She may not be able to draw what she wants, but if she just makes a scribble to represent it, I pick up the thought and act upon it.'

The square is the most magical shape, being the combination of the three plus one – the trinity of spiritual energies plus you! This is what connects you personally to the magical energy that is generated.

Three harnessed into the Magical Square of Transportation

The square is for use when calling great archangels (see also pages 25–28):
Michael for strength, power, courage, determination and protection.
Raphael for healing and communication problems.
Uriel for everything terrestrial, to do with the Earth.
Gabriel for spiritual magic, transformation and difficult, deep-seated emotional problems.

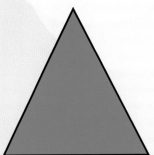

The upper triangle (point upwards) is for all spiritual energy work. In healing with Angel Magic, it represents the energy of the three head chakras – crown, brow and throat (see page 101).

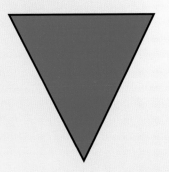

The lower triangle (point downward) represents earthly man, the physical body. In healing with Angel Magic, it represents the energy of the base, sacral and solar plexus chakras. To be used initially when illness is deeply rooted in the physical, for diseases based on rigidity (such as arthritis or bone disease).

Numbers

All numbers are potent tools as their shapes carry a specific energy. The numbers 7, 9, 10 and 12 are esoterically significant numbers to our planetary evolution.

Colours

Colour is used for many aspects of Angel Magic and you should always follow the guides provided. Colours are of particular significance in healing with Angel Magic (see pages 105–107). See also the Rainbow Angels (pages 82–86).

INVOKING THE ANGELS:
MARY'S STORY

Mary was a woman in her late thirties, a lovely person with a husband and a daughter and a good job. Her problem was that she was overweight and had been most of her life. Her weight was not due to overeating and she was quite sensitive about it, especially when seeing medical staff. She had some health problems, had suffered an ectopic pregnancy and had an operation to repair a hernia, which had not been successful and had to be done again. Mary was not worried about the surgery itself, but about the attitude of the consultant she had to see. He was rude, had made comments about her weight in the past and generally undermined her confidence. We decided to work together using Angel Magic.

The day of the appointment arrived and Mary set off very apprehensively. She knew what she had to do but was troubled by her past experience with the consultant, when he had told her that she was lucky to be seen by the NHS being so fat. To Mary's surprise, when she walked into the consultant's office, he greeted her politely, was very pleasant, arranged for her to be admitted into the hospital to have the surgery and made not one single comment about her weight. This man even apologised for the hurt he had caused her during her last visit to the hospital. Her surgery was a success and her confidence is back to normal.

Mary and I had surrounded the consultant with a spiral of pink Angel Light. That's all it took to change this ill-mannered man's attitude towards her.

CRYSTALS

Crystals are things of beauty. They carry a light, energy and information of their own and connect with the Angelic vibration. They can be used to enhance Angel Magic, for healing and clearing. Crystals can clear negative energy. I would recommend the use of clear quartz crystal and rose quartz in most of the rituals.

However, this can be intuitive and people should use crystals they find responsive. Even bowls of coloured glass beads add colour and light and can be useful in enhancing the energy created when working with Angels. Angels will sometimes project their images into crystals.

See page 99 for more details on using crystals.

THE RITUALS

There are guidelines as to when is best for performing Angel Magic and a good rule to remember is: 'Invoke under the waxing Moon; banish under the waning Moon'. At New Moon you can banish first and invoke afterwards, although this will only work on the actual night of the New Moon. At all other times they must be done under the correct phases of the Moon.

The New Moon to the first quarter is the most powerful time for making things grow, flourish and come to fulfilment.

The second day of the full moon to the day of the last quarter is when things worked on will begin to 'die' and pass away.

You can banish as many things as you like. You can invoke for what you really need. But remember that there is a great difference between needing and wanting. Needs are granted, empty desires seldom are. Trust both the angels and your own powers. Approach each magical ritual in a reverential and believing spirit, for you are requesting aid from beings put there by God for your assistance, and the least you can do is to have faith.

The Circular Temple

Guard your mind against evil thoughts impelled by others and bad vibrations by setting up a 'circular temple' each night before you sleep. You do this by imagining a circle of walls, with no doors, which encloses you. Say to yourself, 'Within the temple of my mind no evil thoughts or vibrations can penetrate', and you will soon fall into a restful sleep.

The next day you will find that you can 'see through' people who are trying to upset you or make mischief. Erect the temple of your mind each night before sleep, and you will not only protect yourself, but also allow the angelic powers and wisdom to play through you.

The Creation of Shekinah

'Shekinah' is the Hebrew word for the presence of the Holy Spirit, and is used as the basis of creation of all projects. It is most powerful if created at the time of the New Moon phase, after the Sun sets on Friday (as with the Hebrew start of *Shabbat*, the Sabbath). Make sure that the room you use for this ritual can be left undisturbed for one hour after the blessings. The magic is at its most effective after the creation of Shekinah, but I have found that the rituals do work when there is a need and time is short. Like everything, the more effort one makes the greater the response. However, the Angels can look into our hearts and needs, and right motivation will always be answered.

You will need

An incense stick (as pure as possible)
Ten small candles, tea lights are best, one for each of the following:

- The Cosmic Creator
- The Shekinah
- Anael – Friday
- Cassiel – Saturday
- Uriel – Saturday
- Michael – Sunday
- Gabriel – Monday
- Samael – Tuesday
- Raphael – Wednesday
- Sachiel – Thursday

Pen/pencils
Paper or card

Before you start, make sure that you have all materials to hand. Place the ten candles on a safe surface (where they may be left to burn out), then proceed as follows. Light the incense stick and carry it to each corner of the room, blessing each corner in turn by saying: *In the name of the Cosmic Creator and His angels, I bless this corner.*

Leave the incense stick in a safe holder until it burns out.

Light the first candle and say,
I dedicate this light to the Cosmic Creator.

Draw the Shekinah (see below). Draw the frame carefully from right to left, then top to bottom. Write the letters in the top row first, followed by the letters down the left side and finally the three letters at the bottom right hand corner. Draw as neatly and accurately as you can – remember the greater the effort, the greater the reward.

T	I	P	H	A	R	A	H
I							
P							
H							
A							
R							
A							I
H						I	T

Now light the second candle and say, *I dedicate this light to the Holy Force Field of God and the Archangel Gabriel which is the Shekinah*. Carefully place the Shekinah under or close to the candle.

Now begin lighting the other candles to each of the other angels. The same blessing is said for each angel, naming them and the day they represent.

Candle 3   *Anael, angel of Friday, I dedicate this light to you that your power may work through the Shekinah.*

Candle 4   *Uriel, angel of Saturday, I dedicate this light to you that your power may work through the Shekinah.*

Candle 5   *Cassiel, angel of Saturday, I dedicate this light to you that your power may work through the Shekinah.*

Candle 6   *Michael, angel of Sunday, I dedicate this light to you that your power may work through the Shekinah.*

Candle 7   *Gabriel, angel of Monday, I dedicate this light to you that your power may work through the Shekinah.*

Candle 8   *Samael, angel of Tuesday, I dedicate this light to you that your power may work through the Shekinah.*

Candle 9   *Raphael, angel of Wednesday, I dedicate this light to you that your power may work through the Shekinah.*

Candle 10   *Sachiel, angel of Thursday, I dedicate this light to you that your power may work through the Shekinah.*

Finally, call to Lumiel: *Lumiel, angel of radiance and protection, I call to you that your power may work through the Shekinah.*

To complete the ritual, switch off any electrical lights in the room or shining into the room. Stand quietly in the room for a few minutes, dedicating the room, then leave the room for one hour.

Let the candles burn out of their own accord. When you return to the room, note the difference you feel. Once the candles have burned out, place the Shekinah somewhere safe in the room, preferably where you can see it. You may now carry out all of your other rituals in this room, knowing that they will be enhanced by the power of the Shekinah. This dedication ritual is effective for one week – until exactly the same time next week.

INVOKING THE ANGELS:
MARGARET'S STORY

Margaret came to me very upset and disappointed. Her story was that she had invited several friends and workmates over to her home for a party to celebrate her promotion at work. On her dressing table was her gold chain and cross, an antique that had been her last present from her mother, whom she had recently lost. The chain and cross were valuable but this was not of prime importance, it was insured. The sentimental value was much greater: when she wore the chain she felt that her much-loved mother was with her, there was a tangible presence and somehow it was linked to this chain and cross. The cross and chain disappeared that day. Margaret searched the house from top to bottom, but it was nowhere.

When she contacted me she did not really expect a result but a friend had urged her to make contact. She came to see me on a Thursday and I asked her to call back on Saturday. When she arrived I took her into the room where the Shekinah had been created the day before. Straightaway she commented on the positive feeling in the room. Together we invoked the Archangel Uriel and drew the sign for help in unexpected crises. She took one home to place on her dressing table and I kept one in the special room.

Three or four weeks went by and I had almost forgotten about the matter, when I got a call. Margaret told me that she had found her cross and chain on her dressing table under the lace cloth. She told me that she had taken everything off her dressing table and in fact changed the cloth. Somebody had experienced a change of heart and replaced Margaret's cross and chain. She still does not know who this was and it does not really matter. Margaret's chain and cross are safely around her neck again.

A Prayer for Eternal Peace and Limitless Abundance

The following prayer may be said each morning to
encourage the flow of abundance for all of your needs,
and will be more powerful if said following the
Shekinah ritual. Say it with a pure heart and know that
it will come to pass.

Through the Power of God anchored in my heart and within the hearts of ALL

Humanity, I invoke God's Golden Ray of Eternal Peace and Limitless Abundance.

Precious Sacred Fire, blaze in, through and around every electron of my Being.

Flood my consciousness and the consciousness of every man, woman and child with Eternal Peace and

Limitless Abundance. Lift me into the Realms of Illumined Truth, and bless me with the clear Inner

Knowing that Eternal Peace and the God supply of all good things are my Divine Birthright.

I relinquish now, in the Name of God, all the beliefs I have ever had that are based in poverty consciousness.

In deep humility and gratitude, I consecrate and dedicate my very life to be the open door through which

Eternal Peace and Limitless Abundance will flow to bless me, my family and loved ones, my friends,

co-workers and ALL Humanity.

As I think, speak, feel and act, the Presence of God within me is expanding God's Gift of Eternal Peace

and Prosperity to all life evolving on Earth.

I AM an Awakened Light Being and an Emissary of Love.

I gratefully accept, into my life now, God's Eternal Peace and Limitless Abundance.

And So It is!
Beloved I AM, Beloved I AM, Beloved I AM.
(Anon)

PREPARING FOR THE RITUALS

It is important to prepare the space in which you intend to work the rituals and you can start this process by invoking the assistance of the archangels. Stand in the centre of the room and face each corner in turn as you invoke the support of the four archangels: Raphael, Michael, Gabriel and Uriel.

To the East – Raphael – Air

Great Archangel Raphael, Angel of healing and communication, we call upon thee to come to the East and fill us with the breath of life and the power of Light. Help us to forever join you in singing praises to God. Let our voices in unison rise to the eternal planes.

Great staff bearer of the Divine, empower this work so that it may become a healing force for all and may we always be part of the celestial chorus.'

To the South – Michael – Fire

Great Archangel Michael, Angel of the sun, emissary of the solar logos, and His rays, we call upon thee to come to the South and fill this place with your creative fire, justice and the power of Love.

Michael, 'Perfect of God', Angel of majesty and strength, sword-bearer of the Divine, empower this work so that we may anchor the Divine Light here and brighten all around us.

To the West – Gabriel – Water

Great Archangel Gabriel, Angel of magic and transformation, Angel of the Word of God, we call upon thee to come to the West and fill this place with the waters of life and the knowledge of the Word.

Gabriel, bearer of the cup of the Divine, empower this work and let thy cup overflow with Heaven's Grace and Blessings. May our hearts beat in accord with Divine Resonance.

To the North – Uriel – Earth

Great Archangel Uriel, Angel of the throne, Angel of the Earth, we call upon thee to come to the North and fill this place with peace and stability and the Light of God.

Uriel, bearer of the platter of the Divine, empower this work so that it may overflow with the fruits of the Earth and the abundance of nature.

ANGEL MEDITATION

The following meditation may also help you to relax and get into the right frame of mind to carry out your rituals.

See before you a pathway of golden light. An angel is behind you enfolding you in wings of light. You are being drawn towards the horizon filled with a starlit sky. As you walk towards the glory of this star-filled sky, each star grows brighter and bigger. As you walk along, you become aware of another figure beside you whose body is shining with spiritual brilliance.

You look upon a face that is very familiar and you realise that you are looking at the glory of your higher self, your body of magnificent light. This sacred form stretches out a hand and gently guides you towards a Temple of Light. You are led to a crystal chair and this being of light sits beside you. You may converse with your higher self, your special angel – ask any questions and invoke for any blessings for yourself, those you love and for planetary peace and healing.

Now it is time to leave – give thanks and blessings before you walk out of the temple. You can now return to your familiar surroundings, encircled in a cloak of protection provided for you by your own special angel. See if you are aware of the colour of this cloak. The cloak would signify certain attributes denoted by a special colour. (See chakra colours and significances on pages 101–103.)

INVOKING THE RITUALS

A variety of symbols can be used to invoke the Angels, such as squares, circles and their call signs. To invoke a particular Angel it would be best to use their call sign.

You can invoke the angels by using the symbols of Angel Magic (see page 40). If you know which angel is the correct one for your particular concern, then deal direct with that angel – your Moon course tells you how (see page 62). If you can't work out which angel rules the matter concerned or even if you are forced to 'invent' a symbol, Raphael will understand it and will carry the matter to the appropriate angel for you. When conducting your rituals, don't forget that each day has a guiding angel to whom invocation may be made for help on a particular day (see page 40).

When you work with Angels, remember that everything is an exchange of energy – a two-way flow. Ask, receive gratefully and gracefully, but always give. Give of your energy, your time, your love and your material possessions, when required. This will always be returned tenfold. This two-way flow opens barriers and keeps the energy lines open without any blockages caused by negative thoughts or feelings. When you work with angels a rapport develops and marvellous things happen.

Focus on the symbols and keep them on your person – this strengthens the link. Take them from your pocket or purse each morning and focus your mind on the symbol and the help you are requesting. When you receive that for which you ask, give thanks to the angels and burn the card on which you drew the symbol.

Remember, only invoke for the greatest good of all involved. Never invoke for other reasons, for remember the Great Law of the Universe: 'As it goes around, so it comes around'. Whatever you send out always comes back tenfold!

USING SQUARES

Squares may be drawn on certain nights, depending on the particular ritual, but they will only work after the Shekinah ritual has been performed (see page 65). Remember, the Shekinah is effective from the time it was completed on Friday until the exact time the following Friday. The room in which the Shekinah was created will be the room where you should complete all ritual projects. The particular square must be drawn *exactly* as shown. It is best drawn on card, and where specific colours are mentioned then they are relevant to the ritual. Any deviation to the format will nullify the effect. If you are drawing the square for someone else, and you wish to add specific details, then you must inscribe the details on the reverse in River Script (see page 50).

Raphael

Call upon Raphael for healing, communication and for creative things – all that is new.

Draw the square on any day. Draw on Wednesday to help the animal kingdom.

R	A	P	H	A	E	L
A						E
P						A
H						H
A						P
E						A
L	E	A	H	P	A	R

Michael

Call upon Michael for protection and the power to win spiritual battles; anything to do with strength. Best drawn on Sunday.

Gabriel

Call upon Gabriel for magic, alchemy, transformation and for female/feminine things. This square is particularly helpful for those hoping for a family – to help conceive. Draw on Friday.

M	I	C	H	A	E	L
I						E
C						A
H						H
A						C
E						I
L	E	A	H	C	I	M

G	A	B	R	I	E	L
A						E
B						I
R						R
I						B
E						A
L	E	I	R	B	A	G

Uriel

Call upon Uriel for all material things connecting with spiritual energy; anything for the planet and planetary kingdoms. Draw on Saturday.

U	R	I	E	L
R				E
I				I
E				R
L	E	I	R	U

Cassiel

For roof, (shelter – house, flat, etc) or housing effects. The square is drawn on Saturday to help find, or change, a home (shelter), or to acquire household effects.If you are in doubt, then draw it on both days.

Q	E	N	E	B	A	H
E						A
N						B
E						E
B						N
A						E
H	A	B	E	N	E	Q

HEALING SQUARE TO BRING CALMNESS OR EASE FROM PAIN

The ruler of this square is Raphael – the healer and pain remover. The square may be drawn on any day to dispel pain and help to find peace of mind. It is also for creative things – all that is new.

B	E	B	H	E	R
E	L	E	O	S	
B	E	T	E	M	
H					
E	L	L	O	S	
R					

Draw on a Wednesday to help the animal kingdom. Don't forget – if the request is for someone else or for a specific condition, then the details must be inscribed on the back in River Script.

It is also advisable to use the following Healing Invocation. It may be used both at the time of drawing the Healing Square or at any other appropriate time.

Divine Creator, Eternal Fountain of Life,

send Thy angels of healing, the hosts of Raphael,

to bring wholeness and peace to (name).

Let every muscle, every nerve, every cell, every atom be enfolded

in the light of Thy love.

May the body, mind and soul of (name) be filled with Thy transforming grace,

may the flower of (name)'s heart be open to the power of Thy rays.

Amen.

C	O	S	E	N
O				E
S				C
E				O
N	E	C	O	T

Money-bringing Square

The ruler of this square is Sachiel and it should be drawn on Thursday, when the moon is in good aspect with Jupiter and harmonious with the sun.

The next two squares need to be drawn with particular accuracy as they contain very specific symbols. These are the squares to assist with mental facilities and the Life Protection Chart.

For improvement of mental facilities

For concentration and memory retention, this is good for exams. Raphael is the ruler of this square, which should be drawn on Wednesday. It should be created using black on yellow and kept under the pillow once drawn. It may also be worn as a talisman when sitting an exam or test.

LIFE PROTECTION CHART

This protects the soul from fear and disempowerment, the mind from damage, the body from harm and ill-health. Construct on the day of your moon or sun angel.

It is a good idea to produce one large (A4) square to place in your home, and one small square to carry with you. The colours used when drawing this chart are very specific. Make it on strong white or yellow card. On the reverse side write the name of the person for whom it is being produced in River Script.

 Symbol of fortune: purple

 Physical heart: red

 Star of glory: silver

 Djed of Osiris: gold. (The Djed of Osiris is an ancient Egyptian symbol used to invoke for protection, wisdom and good fortune.)

 Eye of heaven: blue

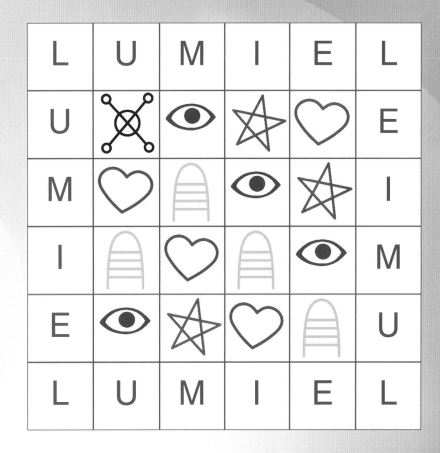

RAINBOW ANGELS

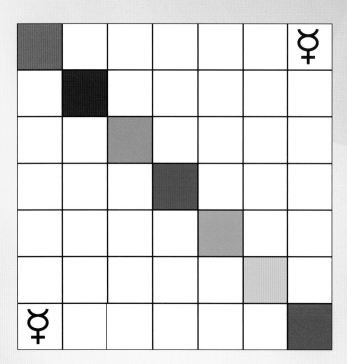

These angels are known as the Angels of the Covenant and can be perceived as translucent coloured light. They resonate with the visible and invisible colours in the spectrum of light and carry all the attributes and qualities of each colour used in creation. Each chakra or energy centre in our bodies resonates to a specific colour which again is represented in the auric field around us. Auras can be clearly seen by some people and represent our thoughts, emotions and aspirations. I believe that our role here is to raise our consciousness and awareness to the highest energy available to us in each energy centre and this again shows in our auras. This is the covenant we have with the Angelic Kingdom and the Rainbow Angels are here to help us achieve this. A diagram of the chakras in the human body with relevant colours and attributes is shown on page 103, and the special functions of the Rainbow Angels using the angel squares appear on the following page. The Rainbow Angels are very beautiful: they link to the planet Venus in our solar system and represent beauty, harmony and fulfilment. They bring happiness and peace, and the visualisation of these angels around us brings a great sense of wellbeing. Each one of us is connected by a stream of energy to the higher worlds, and the Sanskrit term for this connection is *antakarana* which literally translated means 'rainbow bridge'. It is therefore not surprising that Rainbow Angels exist in this energy field around us, and are specifically there to help us connect with higher states of being.

Rainbow Angel squares

Use colour diagonally across from the top left hand corner to the bottom right hand corner. Use a single colour from the spectrum (red, orange, yellow, green, blue, indigo, violet) for specific purposes, or one square of each colour for multi-purposes.

Red

For beginnings. The beginning of the rainbow – empowerment, courage. For stimulating and generating ideas.

Orange

For accessing new horizons. For changes including changes of form or shape – therefore for losing or gaining weight. Also for personal charisma.

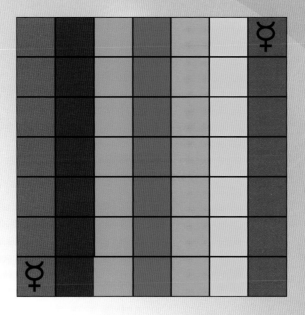

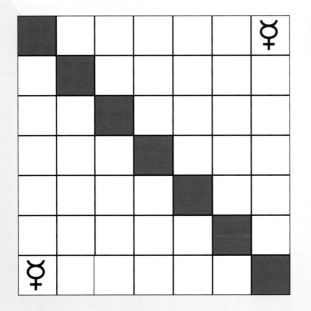

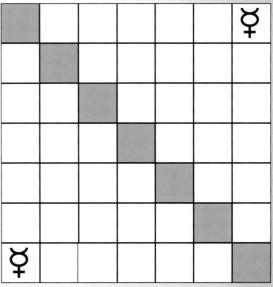

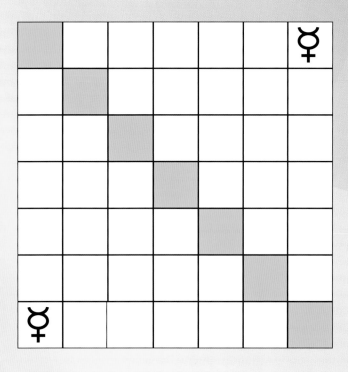

Yellow

For inner health and strength. For power and for anything connected with males or masculine issues.

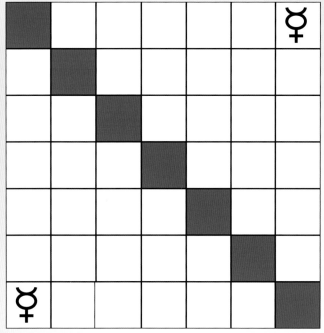

Green

For harmony and balance in all areas of life. For anything connected with nature. For all environmental issues. For your own personal environment. For changes. For acceptance of situations.

Blue

For recharging your batteries. For health problems. For sensitivity – physical, mental and emotional.

Indigo

For discernment, discrimination, psychic gifts, clairvoyance, etc. For problems with eyesight, or for a clear view of difficult or tricky situations.

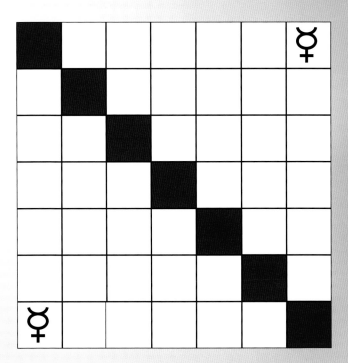

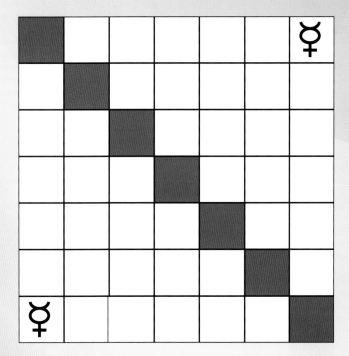

Violet

For all spiritual gifts and achievements. For total healing especially when causes for illness are rooted in the past. For emotional problems. For family matters.

Summary

RED — for determination, courage, beginnings, stimulating actions.

ORANGE — for change in all areas of life, for personal warmth and charisma, for changing thought patterns, for help with addictions.

YELLOW — for inner growth, mental stimulation, for general well-being, for the power in nature.

GREEN — for energy, harmony, for new creations, new projects.

BLUE — for healing, for mental sensitivity, for re-charging of energy, for spiritual understanding.

INDIGO — inner vision, release of pressurised situations, raising of energy levels, for discernment and discrimination.

VIOLET — for ultimate balance of body, mind and spirit, for clearing of all negative situations, for spiritual gifts, also for holistic health, for harmony in all areas.

INVOKING THE ANGELS:
SARAH'S STORY

Sarah was a clever girl, who excelled in all her routine schoolwork, was active in the classroom but went to pieces during exams. She had never managed to pass an exam and was thinking of leaving school without sitting for any examinations. She had tried counselling, her teachers had done their best but nothing worked. Sarah's mother came to see me and asked if I could help. Sarah and I had a few meetings and I explained to her about the power of the angels and its effect on us and how the help was there for us, provided we did our bit. She was a little sceptical but decided to try. She drew the mirror of the mind square on the Wednesday before her first exam, kept a version under her pillow and carried another in her pocket. That was the first exam Sarah passed and she has had no trouble since. Sarah now talks to her angels and receives their help in all areas of her life.

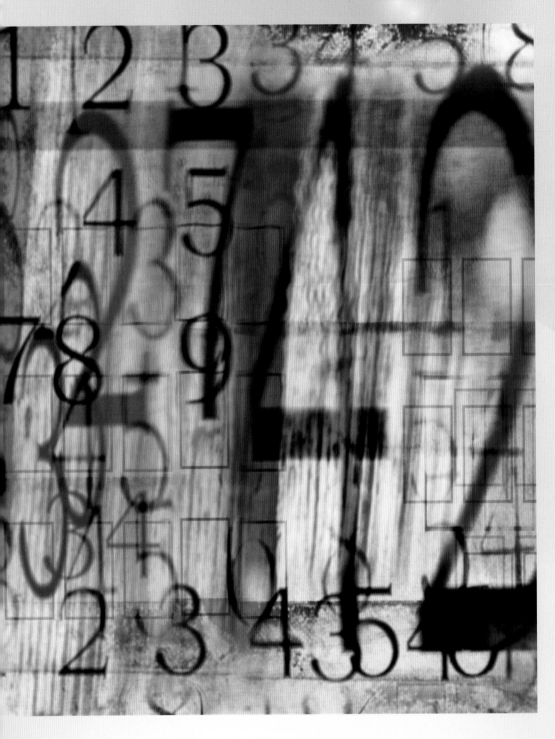

The number of ritual squares that can be drawn is limited only by your scope of imagination. There is an old saying, 'necessity is the mother of invention', and this rule applies equally to the use of Angel Magic. Let your heart guide you and give your imagination free rein. It is the intent that is important. If you let your intuition guide you, your angels will understand the symbolism of the call. Don't forget, if you want to include a message to clarify the detail of your request or if you wish to make the request for someone else, write the details or name on the back of the square or symbol in either River or Theban Script.

USING OTHER SYMBOLS

Angels recognise all symbols – they are universal (see page 54). A few are shown below to cover aspects of help required by most of us at some time. In each case, focus on the issue or assistance required, ask the right angel for help, draw the symbol on a piece of card and carry it with you until you get what you have asked for.

For material help call on Sachiel and Samael, ideally on Thursday or at the time of the New Moon.

For increased clairvoyance and spiritual abilities call on Asariel on Thursday.

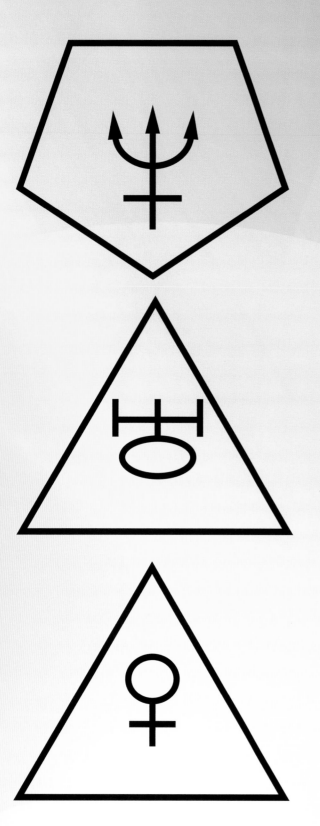

For help or inspiration with a project call on Anael on Friday.

For healing or help with communications, letters, or documents call on Raphael on Wednesday.

For help with unexpected crises call on Uriel on Saturday.

INVOKING THE ANGELS:
DAVID AND ANN'S STORY

David and Ann were on six months' holiday in Australia, with a view to researching whether it was the right country for them to make a fresh start in. They were enjoying themselves, had prepared very well, had researched the areas they were travelling in and had also prepared their life protection charts. They were on their way to a motel in Kempsey, New South Wales, en route from Sydney, driving up to the Gold Coast. They had stopped for a light lunch and intended driving until they reached the motel. It was a bit later than they had anticipated and there was a storm. It was pouring with rain and driving conditions were less than ideal. Ann suddenly felt she should telephone the motel and inform them that they would be arriving late, so they made a mutual decision to stop at the next rest place and make their call using their mobile phone.

Both of them suddenly had this overwhelming urge for a cup of coffee and there was a sign for a roadhouse coming up. They pulled in, went for a coffee and made the call to the motel there. They then got back into the car and started driving. As they neared the signs for the rest place they had originally planned to stop in, they saw police cars and ambulances. A large truck had crashed, hitting several cars and there appeared to be quite a few people hurt. Some of them were being taken away by ambulance. As they slowly drove past they realised that they would have been parked there at the time of the accident. Ann said, 'I felt so sorry for the people and so grateful for our safety, and the angelic symbols just flashed into my mind. I knew we had been taken care of'.

HEALING WITH ANGEL LIGHT

HEALING WITH ANGEL LIGHT

As we move further into this period of our planetary history, I am told that we are moving into the age of transformation. This will be a period when many cosmic gifts and powers, so far latent in man, will be activated to enable humanity as a whole to move forward into the next stage of our spiritual evolution. Great changes are and will be taking place, most of them in our own awareness. We will be given the ability to see with our inner vision, to discern with the higher mind and to feel with a heart of unconditional love.

Much will be brought into the domain of scientists working in many areas. They will begin to see that there are higher laws that supersede all the known physical laws that have been learnt and understood over the centuries. Fixed ideas will be upturned and many a so-called 'truth' will be exposed for the illusion it is. We will be required to move away from orthodox ways of handling illness and disease. We need to allow the natural divine energies that abound in the universe and in every life form to flow freely and not be hampered by barriers of fear, doubt and negativity. The mind is a very important tool and, aligned to the Divine Mind, it is the highest force in the manifested universe.

TRANSFER OF ENERGY RADIANCE (TER) HEALING TECHNIQUE

This TER technique was first given to me in a dream and later endorsed in meditation. The masters I work with assured me that it will become a very effective tool for healing. I pass it on with love and trust.

This technique involves Divine Radiation being channelled through you, a radiation that can be enhanced using colour (see page 105), using specific sacred shapes (see page 54); using sacred sounds, chants, mantras and resonance (see page 49) and using crystals (see page 99).

State of mind is the first thing that needs to be altered. Release all fears, doubts, negative feelings, and non-forgiveness and let a feeling of well-being take over, confident in the generosity and abundance of the creative energy. A good way of activating this state is to work on the 12 electromagnetic fields that connect us to the more subtle realms of life.

Take 12 deep breaths, consciously breathing in God's love and Angel Light, and releasing all negative energy into the Earth. After this you need to activate your own centres of radiance – we have three major centres: the heart, the eyes, and the palms. It is advisable to take six breaths for each centre. As a channel for higher vibratory energy, the light quotient in your cells increases and this light, when activated in service, becomes radiation – a radiatory energy with great restorative and transformational qualities.

Now you are ready to use this radiant energy for healing or any other purpose to aid your fellow , or in fact any other life form, animal, plant, or mineral.

Always bring the energy through the crown into the heart then out via the heart, eyes and palms of the hands. Work simultaneously to emit radiatory energy from all these points to the person or animal you are healing.

When using the TER technique you will get an intuitive feeling regarding which symbol is most appropriate for the person concerned. Follow your intuitive response after preparing. Always work through your heart: feel the energy flowing into your crown and out through your heart. Cultivate thoughts of love.

When using a crystal, the energy is directed into the crystal and then into the recipient. The crystal should be placed between the healer and the patient. To achieve the best results, after the preparation procedure and activation of the 12 electromagnetic energy fields, place the crystal and any shape, (if required) visualise a colour, if appropriate, and start the healing process, slowly radiating energy to the patient via the three radiatory centres.

This can be followed by a laying-on of hands, first touching the patient's heart, then placing hands over their eyes, and then palm to palm. Should the patient prefer not to be touched, the same effect can be achieved placing the hands a few inches above these areas. After working in this way, move the hands to the chakra closest to the area which needs healing and work on the area itself.

Ideally, a session should take about half an hour, but this can be varied according to need. This technique can also be used in distant healing and is very effective when visualising the patient during the healing session.

Sounds music and sacred mantras can be played to help focus the mind, while the acoustical vibration activates the centres, enabling them to emit and receive the radiatory energy more effectively.

The effort required will depend largely on the severity and root cause of the disease. Most problems will begin to respond after three sessions, when the patient should feel better able to cope and pain should lessen. As in all forms of healing, the result is dependent on many factors. Healing of any sort does not guarantee a cure but the condition will always be helped, and in many cases a cure is effected.

With the healing of animals, particularly domestic pets, the square should be used, activating the angelic vibration. The 'Deva' and elemental kingdom, part of the angelic kingdom, are closely involved in the care of the animal and plant kingdoms and respond to vibration. The colours best used are green or blue. The latter is a universal healing colour and green is the colour of nature, of harmony and balance, and carries a truly restorative energy. It is the best colour to use for animal healing. Devas are spirit Beings of Light belonging to the Angel family who work with Angels. Most mature trees and plants have resident Devas, as do animals. Even great buildings have Devas.

For planetary healing it is best to use the colour associated with the ray energy flowing into the planet at this time. As we are under the energy and vibration of the seventh ray, ceremonial order of magic, the colour is violet. This is a very effective colour for the dispersal and transformation of negative energy. Use for all types of universal healing or for work associated with transformation and change, for example, for altering states of hostility and tension.

In planetary healing, one uses prayer, invocation, healing techniques and Angel Magic for helping large areas of the planet or the whole planet, in the case of war or natural disasters. The same techniques can be used, but the focus will then be on the planet or part of it. 'Mother Earth' or the name of any individual country could be inscribed in one of the scripts on the reverse of the square or whatever symbol is used.

HEALING WITH CRYSTALS

Crystals may be charged for any spiritual work connected with the energy of an angel. Use the same method each time.

Charging Crystals

Light three candles and place them in a triangular formation. Put the crystal for charging in the middle of the triangle. Sit quietly for a few minutes and then call down the radiant energy of the archangel in question. See the energy flowing into the triangle created by the candles, and entering the crystal, charging it with the highest healing angelic vibration and light. Say the appropriate words (see below) and leave the candles burning until they go out by themselves.

Lord Raphael, charge this crystal with your healing light, and make it a Divine tool that I may use for transferring your radiant healing energy.

Calling Raphael increases the light power of the crystal. He should be called to bring light and healing.

For protection and spiritual growth
Lord Michael, charge this crystal with your immense light for my protection and the protection of others. Please enhance our ability to understand the Divine mind, the Divine plan and the role we need to play to bring the plan into fruition.

For all earthly help
Lord Uriel, charge this crystal with your radiant energy so

that I may use it for all earthly matters, to help myself and others.

For transformation, spiritual magic and understanding new energies
Lord Gabriel, charge this crystal with your energy of spiritual magic and transformation, help us to work with new energies to change our material aspects to spiritual ones.

The crystals can now be used in many ways and need to be treated in a respectful way. Carry your crystal with you if you can, and let your intuition guide you as to its use.

Crystal Angel Light Healing

Use your charged healing crystal. The person to be healed may either hold the crystal or have it placed near them. In absent healing, write the person's name on a piece of paper and place it under the crystal. Light a candle.

CHAKRAS

Chakras are energy centres located in the human body. The word 'chakra' is Sanskrit and means 'spinning wheel'. They are spiritual energy centres, with spiral openings which allow energy to enter and to flow out of their vortices.

The seven major chakras are depicted. We do however have others, for example in the palms of our hands. This is how we can transmit energy for healing through our hands.

The chakras link the physical body, the ethereal body, the emotional body and the mental body. Each chakra is responsible for a particular area, a specific gland, a colour and an effective crystal is associated with it.

The Angels use these energy centres to assist us in refining the energy we produce and enable us to receive spiritual energy.

Call upon Archangel Raphael and the ministering healing angels and ask for their help. Say out loud, *Great Archangel Raphael, I call down your sacred energy and crystal light to assist in this healing process.*
Visualise a pyramid of light from the source of God, from which three great streams of light flow into Archangel Raphael and the healing angels. They in turn send down rays of light to the person being healed.

See the light spiralling down in crystal drops entering the crown chakra, fill that area with spirals of light and see all negativity and old thought forms disappear. Use the crystal light to release old negative thought forms, as the spirals of light energy push the unwanted thoughts out, and allow the original perfect thought forms to grow.

Work through all the chakras focusing on each one in turn, and flooding each one with spirals of crystal light. After the crown, work on the brow chakra, then the throat, taking your time and focusing on each one for a few minutes.

After the throat, move to the heart chakra, the solar plexus, the sacral, and finally the chakra at the base of the spine. Visualise your patient's spine as a pillar of light with spirals of angelic crystal light flowing down all around it. Always remember to thank the angels at the end of your healing. Remember healing may not always cure the condition, but it will always help with pain relief, the state of mind and the person's ability to cope with the disease.

THE CHAKRAS.

There is a colour chart connected with the chakra points in the body. Each chakra has a colour assigned to it. You will need to be aware of these colours, particularly when requesting Angel Healing with colours.

CROWN CHAKRA VIOLET

BROW CHAKRA INDIGO

THROAT CHAKRA BLUE

HEART CHAKRA GREEN

SOLAR PLEXUS CHAKRA
(just above navel) yellow

SACRAL CHAKRA
(just below navel) orange

BASE CHAKRA
(base of spine) red

INVOKING THE ANGELS:
PETER'S STORY

A good friend of mine, who lives in Germany, telephoned me and he said he was really afraid. His spine was in a very inflamed and painful state, he could hardly walk and, for the second time, his doctor had recommended an injection delivered under X-ray right into the nerves of the spine. The effect of the injection was to stop the pain and he said the effect was good but the injection itself was excruciatingly painful. It only lasted a few minutes but was agony: they could not use an anaesthetic of any sort. I asked him a few questions and established the day and approximate time of his appointment at the hospital, which he told me was in the morning between 10am and 11am.

That day I called upon the Archangel Raphael and the healing angels and visualised the healing Angel Light pouring down Peter's spine. I kept the flow going for about twenty minutes, drew the healing sign, put Peter's name in the river script on the reverse and placed it under my healing crystal.

The following day I telephoned Peter. He was free of pain and said to me, 'It was amazing. I did not feel the injection at all. The previous time was unbearably painful and I was dreading having to go through it again.
Thank you so much.'

ANGEL LIGHT HEALING
WITH COLOUR

Use a healing crystal in the same
way as with healing with crystals
(see page 99). Call down Archangel
Raphael and the ministering healing
angels and ask for their help. Say out
loud, *Great Archangel Raphael and the
healing colour angels, please send down
your sacred energy and coloured crystal
light to assist this healing process.*

Visualise a pyramid of light from the
source of God, out of which flows
three streams of light into Archangel
Raphael and the healing angels.

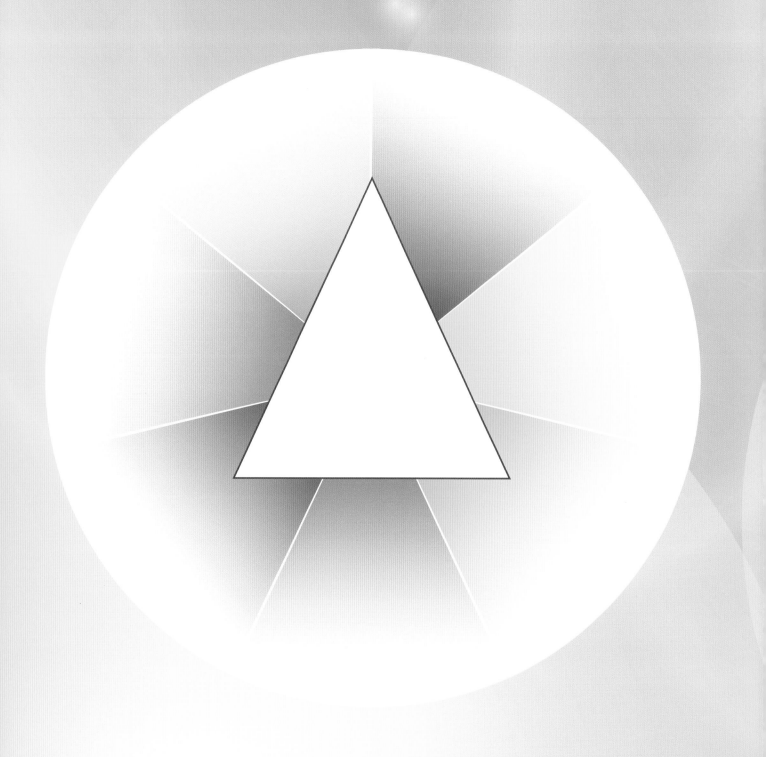

The angels in turn send down seven rays of coloured light. Feel this light spiralling down in crystal drops of colour:

Take the violet light to the crown chakra and flood the whole area with violet light. Focus for a few minutes.

Take the indigo light to the brow chakra and flood the whole area with indigo light. Focus for a few minutes.

Take the blue light to the throat chakra and flood the whole area with blue light. Focus for a few minutes.

Take the green light to the heart chakra and flood the whole area with green light. Focus for a few minutes.

Take the yellow light to the solar plexus chakra and flood the whole area with yellow light. Focus for a few minutes.

Take the orange light to the sacral chakra and flood the whole area with orange light. Focus for a few minutes.

Take the red light to the base chakra and flood the whole area with red light. Focus for a few minutes.

Now visualise your patient's spine as a pillar of coloured light, a rainbow bridge connecting to the Divine.

Hold the focus for a little while; the coloured light will turn to white light as the healing draws to an end.

Always remember to thank the angels at the end of the healing. This technique can be used very effectively for oneself as well as others.

AFTERWORD

The universe abounds with magic and all these things open doorways through which the magical energies can reach us and those for whom we invoke.

For those of you who wish to see an angelic being or elemental, either when meditating or in a dream at night, draw the following square and hold it in your hand while meditating or place it under your pillow.

If you wish to see a special angel, then draw the square and the call sign of the angel in the top left-hand corner. Write the name of the angel overleaf using one of the scripts.

When you work with love and good intention you are completely protected, and you attract to you that which you are giving out. Good and positive will only attract good and positive responses. Writing the name of the angel for this ritual is very specific, in order to see a special Angel, by that I mean one in particular.

Talk to your angels and allow them to open a pathway of love and light to God's domain, the heavenly realms, so that all God's creatures will move into a higher spiritual dimension where all will live in love and unity of purpose. Truly, God's Divine plan for humanity and all other kingdoms will be reborn on our planet Earth.

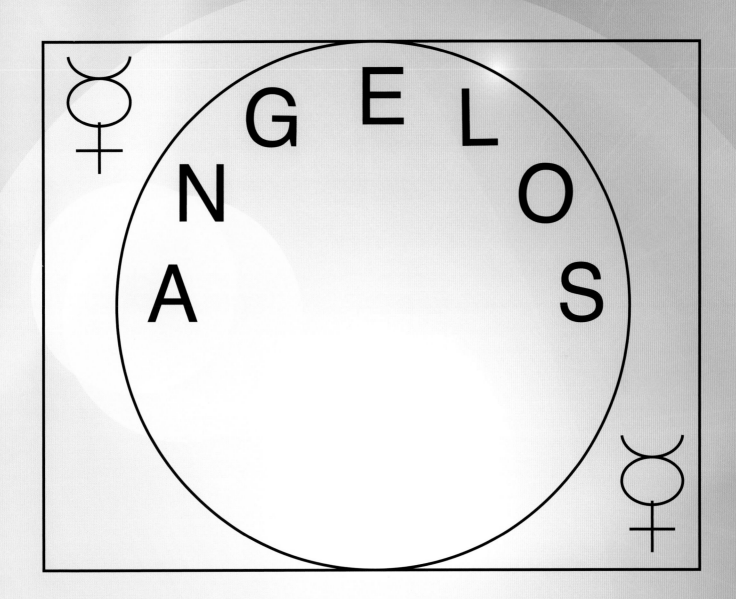

INDEX

ACKNOWLEDGEMENTS

David Conway: *Magic – The Complete Do-It-Yourself Guide,* Jonathan Cape Ltd., 1972.

A.D. Luk: *Law of Life* A.D. Luk Publications. 1960. Pueblo.

Madeleine Montalban, for the Theban and River Scripts

Crystalinks http://www.crystalinks.com

Spirit-Web Internet Site This site, spiritweb.org run by Rene Mueller closed down in Aug 2003.

Over the years I have attended various esoteric courses and seminars, and give thanks for guidance to Theosophical Literature, Dr Douglas Baker, Alton Kamadon and many others, too numerous to mention.

Picture credits

Illustrations pp6, 8, 18, 20-23, 25-34, 36-37, 42-44, 47, 60, 71-72, 74, 76-78, 92, 105

by David Ashby

Images pp7, 10, 12, 24, 3-39, 46, 54, 56, 62, 64, 67-68, 73, 75, 88, 96-99 © Getty Images

Image p94 © Stockbyte

Photographs pp59, 96, 99-100 by Colin Bowling